To My Angels: Keep reading, keep dreaming, keep writing, keep creating—you are my world!

www.mascotbooks.com

Fat Tuesday

For more information, please contact:
Mascot Books
620 Herndon Parkway, Suite 320
Herndon, VA 20170
info@mascotbooks.com

Library of Congress Control Number: 2019920085

CPSIA Code: PRT0520A
ISBN-13: 978-1-64543-333-0

Printed in the United States

Fat Tuesday

by **Angel Stull-James**

Illustrated by Ingrid Lefebvre

We don't see her as much, and for now she's a ghost.
So we bid her a special cheers along with a toast.

No Tuesday Bluesday
practices like her
F18 jet squad,

But she travels with them like peas in a pod.

Part of the United States Navy in her gold, white, and blue,

But flown only by United States Marines, yes, it is true.

U.S. Navy and U.S. Marines, Bert carries them both.

She's the most famous C130 Transport plane flying coast to coast.

Performing for millions across the country,
she has seen her fair share of crowd-favored love,
With her red, white, and blue American flag
waving proudly above.

A Hercules, strong and adventurous, like the mythical god, heroic even, and flying high in the sky.

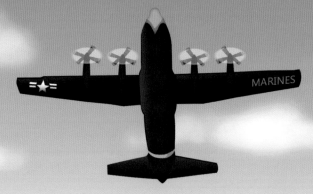

Tasked with bringing our fallen Angel home for one last salute and Pensacola flyby.

She's big and she's fierce but not as often seen.

She's beloved and iconic and brings home
the Blue Angels team.

On Sunday evenings as we watch the sky for her, "Fat Albert!!!" we cheer,

Waving frantically in excitement the more she comes near!

For years she has called Pensacola, Florida her home,

But now off to the Lone Star State she has flown.

She's taken to the blue skies for the last time in May.

Goodbye and farewell, and "We love you Fat Albert!" we say.

"Safe retirement big girl, and for the safe arrival of your new sister," we pray.

The End

Also by Angel Stull-James

Tuesday Bluesday

Angel Stull-James is a native of
Pensacola, Florida, and honored graduate
of Florida State University. Angel is a
former model and actress and worked in the
fashion industry in New York City. Angel
is a licensed mediator in Florida and a
licensed attorney in Florida and New York.
Angel's greatest accomplishment, however,
is being a mother. Her children are her
inspiration and her motivation. Angel seeks to inspire her
children to follow their dreams just as they have inspired her to follow hers.

Fat Tuesday is the second book of many that Angel has written for her
children, to be included in her desired children's book series about the
world-famous United States Navy Blue Angels. Following in suit, the rhymes
in *Fat Tuesday* are a fun read, not only for young children, but for any Fat
Albert and Blue Angels fans of all ages.

Autographs

Autographs

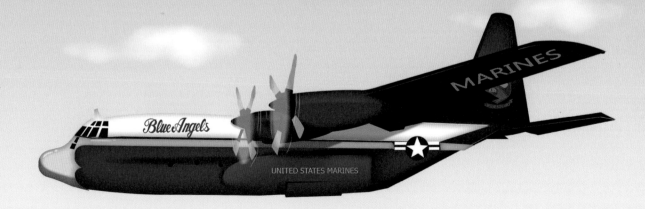